Osho taught philosophy at the University of Jabalpur before establishing the commune in Poona, India, which has become famous all over the world as a mecca for seekers wanting to experience meditation and transformation. His teachings have influenced millions of people of all ages and from all walks of life. He has been described by the *Sunday Times* as one of the 1,000 makers of the 20th century, and by *The Sunday Mid-Day* (India) as one of the ten people – along with Gandhi, Nehru and Buddha – who have changed the destiny of India.

what is MEDITATION?

osho

ELEMENT

Shaftesbury, Dorset • Rockport, Massachusetts
Brisbane, Queensland

© Osho International Foundation 1995

This edition published in Great Britain in 1995 by
Element Books Limited
Shaftesbury, Dorset

Published in the USA in 1995 by
Element, Inc.
42 Broadway, Rockport, MA 01966

Published in Australia in 1995 by
Element Books Limited
for Jacaranda Wiley Limited
33 Park Road, Milton, Brisbane 4064

Editing: Ma Deva Sarito
Design: Ma Dhyan Amiyo
Cover Illustration by Orange

Printed and bound in Great Britain by
Hartnolls, Bodmin, Cornwall

British Library Cataloguing in Publication
data available

Library of Congress Cataloging in Publication
data available

ISBN 1-85230-726-9

what is MEDITATION?

THE WORLD WAS very different in the past, obviously. About six weeks' worth of sensory stimuli six hundred years ago is what we now get in a day. Six weeks' worth of stimulation, information, we are getting *Introduction* in a single day – about forty times the pressure to learn and adapt. Modern man has to be capable of learning more than man has ever been before, because there is more to learn now. Modern man has to become capable of adapting to new situations every day because the world is changing so fast. It is a great challenge.

A great challenge, if accepted, will help tremendously in the expansion of consciousness. Either modern man is going to be utterly neurotic or modern man is going to be transformed by the very pressure. It depends on how you take it. One thing is certain: there is no way of going back. The sensory stimuli will go on increasing more and more. You will be getting more and more information and life will be changing with faster and faster rhythms. And you will have to be capable of learning, of adapting to new things.

In the past man lived in an almost static world. Everything was static. You would leave the world exactly as your father had left it to you, you would not have changed anything at all. Nothing was changed, there was no question of learning too much. A little bit of learning was enough and then you had spaces in your mind, empty spaces, which helped people to remain sane.

Now there is no more empty space unless you create it deliberately.

Meditation is needed today more than ever before. Meditation is needed so much that it is almost a question of life and death. In the past it was a luxury; few people — a Buddha, a Mahavira, a Krishna — were interested in it. Other people were naturally silent, naturally happy, sane. There was no need for them to think of meditation; in an unconscious way they were meditating. Life was moving so silently, moving so slowly, that even the most stupid people were capable of adapting to it. Now the change is so tremendously fast, with such speed, that even the most intelligent people feel incapable of adapting to it. Every day life is different, and you have to learn again — you have to learn and learn again and again. You can never stop learning now; it has to be a life-long process. To the very point of death you will have to remain a learner, only then can you remain sane, can you avoid neurosis. And the pressure is great — forty times greater.

How to relax this pressure? You will have to go deliberately into meditative moments. If a person is not meditating at least one hour a day, then neurosis will not be accidental, he will create it himself.

For one hour he should disappear from the world into his own being. For one hour he should be so alone that nothing penetrates him — no memory, no thought, no imagination; for one hour no content in his consciousness, and that will rejuvenate him and that will refresh him. That will release new sources of energy in him and he will be back in the world, younger, fresher, more able to learn, with more wonder in his eyes, with more awe in his heart — again a child.

Osho, The Secret of Secrets,

what is MEDITATION?

MEDITATION IS NOT anything of the mind, it is something beyond the mind. And the first step is to be playful about it. If you are playful about it

meditation is PLAYFUL

mind cannot destroy your meditation. Otherwise it will turn it into another ego trip; it will make you very serious. You will start thinking, 'I am a great meditator. I am holier than other people, and the whole world is just worldly – I am religious, I am virtuous.' That's what has happened to thousands of so-called saints, moralists, puritans: they are just playing ego games, subtle ego games.

Hence I want to cut the very root of it from the very beginning. Be playful about it. It is a song to be sung, a dance to be danced. Take it as fun and you will be surprised: if you can be playful about meditation, meditation will grow in leaps and bounds.

But you are not hankering for any goal; you are just enjoying sitting silently, just enjoying the very act of sitting silently – not that you are longing for some yogic powers, *siddhis,* miracles. All that is nonsense, the same old nonsense, the same old game, played with new words, on a new plane....

Life as such has to be taken as a cosmic joke – and then suddenly you relax because there is nothing to be tense about. And in that very relaxation something starts changing in you – a radical change, a transformation – and the small things of life start having new meaning, new significance. Then nothing is small, everything starts taking on a new flavor, a new aura; one starts feeling a kind of godliness everywhere. One does not become a Christian, does not become a Hindu, does not become a Mohammedan; one simply becomes a lover of life. One learns only one thing, how to rejoice in life.

But rejoicing in life is the way towards god. Dance your way to god, laugh your way to god, sing your way to god! [1]

YOU HAVE LIVED in a certain way up to now – don't you want to live in a different way? You have thought in a certain way up to now – don't

meditation is CREATIVE you want some new glimpses in your being?

Then be alert and don't listen to the mind.

Mind is your past constantly trying to control your present and your future. It is the dead past which goes on controlling the alive present. Just become alert about it.

But what is the way? How does the mind go on doing it? The mind does it with this method: it says, 'If you don't listen to me, you will not be as efficient as I am. If you do an old thing you can be more efficient because you have done it before. If you do a new thing you cannot be so efficient. The mind goes on talking like an economist, an efficiency expert; it goes on saying, 'This is easier to do. Why do it the hard way? This is the way of least resistance.'

Remember, whenever you have two things, two alternatives, choose the new one. Choose the harder, choose the one in which more awareness will be needed. At the cost of efficiency always choose awareness, and you will create the situation in which meditation will become possible. These are all just situations. Meditation will happen – I am not saying that just by doing them you will get to meditation, but they will be helpful. They will create the necessary situation in you, without which meditation cannot happen.

Be less efficient but more creative. Let that be the motive. Don't be bothered too much about utilitarian ends. Rather, constantly remember that you are not here in life to become a commodity. You are not here to become a utility, that is below dignity. You are not here just to become more and more efficient. You are here to become more and more alive; you are here to become more and more intelligent; you are here to become more and more happy, ecstatically happy. But that is totally different from the ways of the mind. [2]

WHATSOEVER YOU DO, do it with deep alertness; then even small things become sacred. Then cooking or cleaning become sacred; they become worship. It is not a question of what you are doing, the question is *how* you are doing it. You can clean the floor like a robot, a mechanical thing; you have to clean it, so you clean it. Then you miss something beautiful. Then you waste those moments in only cleaning the floor. Cleaning the floor could have been a great experience; you missed it. The floor is cleaned but something that could have happened within you has not happened. If you were aware, not only the floor but you would have felt a deep cleansing. Clean the floor full of awareness, luminous with awareness. Work or sit or walk, but one thing has to be a continuous thread: make more and more moments of your life luminous with awareness. Let the candle of awareness burn in each moment, in each act. The cumulative effect is what enlightenment is. The cumulative effect, all the moments together, all small candles together, become a great source of light. [3]

meditation is ALERTNESS

WHAT IS MEDITATION? Is it a technique that can be practiced? Is it an effort that you have to do? Is it something which the mind can achieve? It is not. All that the mind can do cannot be *meditation is* YOUR NATURE meditation – it is something beyond the mind, the mind is absolutely helpless there. The mind cannot penetrate meditation; where mind ends, meditation begins. This has to be remembered, because in our life, whatsoever we do, we do through the mind; whatsoever we achieve, we achieve through the mind. And then, when we turn inwards, we again start thinking in terms of techniques, methods, doings, because the whole of life's experience shows us that everything can be done by the mind. Yes – except meditation, everything can be done by the mind. Everything is done by the mind except meditation. Because meditation is not an achieve-ment – it is already the case, it is your nature. It has not to be achieved; it has only to be recognized, it has only to be remembered. It is there waiting for you – just a turning in, and it is available. You have been carrying it always and always.

Meditation is your intrinsic nature – it is you, it is your being, it has nothing to do with your doings. You cannot have it and you cannot not have it. It cannot be possessed, it is not a thing. It is you. It is your being. [4]

WHEN PEOPLE COME to me and they ask, "How to meditate?" I tell them, "There is no need to ask how to meditate, just ask how to remain unoccupied.

***meditation is* NON-DOING** Meditation happens spontaneously. Just ask how to remain unoccupied, that's all. That's the whole trick of meditation – how to remain unoccupied. Then you cannot do anything. The meditation will flower.

When you are not doing anything the energy moves towards the center, it settles down towards the center. When you are doing something the energy moves out. Doing is a way of moving out.

Non-doing is a way of moving in. Occupation is an escape. You can read the Bible, you can make it an occupation. There is no difference between religious occupation and secular occupation: all occupations are occupations, and they help you to cling outside your being. They are excuses to remain outside.

Man is ignorant and blind, and he wants to remain ignorant and blind, because to come inwards looks like entering into a chaos. And it is so; inside you have created a chaos. You have to encounter it and go through it. Courage is needed – courage to be oneself, and courage to move inwards. I have not come across a greater courage than that – the courage to be meditative.

But people who are engaged outside – with worldly things or nonworldly things, but occupied all the same, they think ... and they have created a rumor around it, they have their own philoso-phers. They say that if you are an introvert you are somehow morbid, something is wrong with you. And they are in the majority. If you meditate, if you sit silently, they will joke about you: "What are you doing? – gazing at your navel? What are you doing? – opening the third eye? Where are you going? Are you morbid?... because what is there to do inside? There is nothing inside."

Inside doesn't exist for the majority of people, only the outside exists. And just the opposite is the case – only inside is real; outside is nothing but a dream. But they call introverts morbid, they call meditators morbid. In the West they think that the East is a little morbid. What is the point of sitting alone and looking inwards? What are you going to get there? There is nothing.

David Hume, one of the great British philosophers, tried once... because he was studying the Upanishads and they go on saying: Go in, go in, go in – that is their only message. So he tried it. He closed his eyes one day – a totally secular man, very logical, empirical, but not meditative at all – he closed his eyes and he said, "It is so boring! It is a boredom to look in. Thoughts move, sometimes a few emotions, and they go on racing in the mind, and you go on looking at them – what is the point of it? It is useless. It has no utility."

And this is the understanding of many people. Hume's standpoint is that of the majority: What are you going to get inside? There is darkness, thoughts floating here and there. What will you do? What will come out of it? If Hume had waited a little longer – and that is difficult for such people – if he had been a little more patient, by and by thoughts disappear, emotions subside. But if it had happened to him he would have said, "That is even worse, because emptiness comes. At least first there were thoughts, something to be occupied with, to look at, to think about. Now even thoughts have disappeared; only emptiness.... What to do with emptiness? It is absolutely useless."

But if he had waited a little more, then darkness also disappears. It is just like when you come from the hot sun and you enter your house: everything looks dark because your eyes need a little attunement. They are fixed on the hot sun outside; comparatively, your house looks dark. You cannot see, you feel as if it is night. But you wait, you sit, you rest in a chair, and after a few seconds the eyes get attuned. Now it is not dark, a little more light....

You rest for an hour, and everything is light, there is no darkness at all.

If Hume had waited a little longer, then darkness also disappears. Because you have lived in the hot sun outside for many lives your eyes have become fixed, they have lost the flexibility. They need tuning. When one comes inside the house it takes a little while, a little time, a patience. Don't be in a hurry.

In haste nobody can come to know himself. It is a very very deep awaiting. Infinite patience is needed. By and by darkness disappears. There comes a light with no source. There is no flame in it, no lamp is burning, no sun is there. A light, just like it is in the morning: the night has disappeared, and the sun has not risen.... Or in the evening – the twilight, when the sun has set and the night has not yet descended. That's why Hindus call their prayer time *sandhya*. *Sandhya* means twilight, light without any source.

When you move inwards you will come to the light without any source. In that light, for the first time you start understanding yourself, who you are, because you are that light. You are that twilight, that *sandhya,* that pure clarity, that perception, where the observer and the observed disappear, and only the light remains. [5]

MEDITATION STARTS BY being separate from the mind, by being a witness. That is the only way of separating yourself from anything. If you are looking at the light, *meditation is* WITNESSING naturally one thing is certain: you are not the light, you are the one who is looking at it. If you are watching the flowers, one thing is certain: you are not the flower, you are the watcher.

Watching is the key of meditation:

Watch your mind.

Don't do anything – no repetition of a mantra, no repetition of the name of god – just watch whatever the mind is doing. Don't disturb it, don't prevent it, don't repress it; don't do anything at all on your part. You just be a watcher, and the miracle of watching is meditation. As you watch, slowly, slowly mind becomes empty of thoughts; but you are not falling asleep, you are becoming more alert, more aware.

As the mind becomes completely empty, your whole energy becomes a flame of awakening. This flame is the result of meditation. So you can say meditation is another name of watching, witnessing, observing - without any judgment, without any evaluation. Just by watching, you immediately get out of the mind....

Whatever Maharishi Mahesh Yogi and other people like him are doing is good, but they are calling something meditation which is not. That's where they are leading people astray. If they had remained sincere and authentic and told people that this will give you mental health, physical health, a more relaxed life, a more peaceful existence, it would have been right. But once they started calling it 'transcendental meditation' they have raised a very trivial thing to an ultimate significance which it cannot fulfill. People have been in transcendental meditation for years, and in the East, for thousands of years. But that has not become their self-knowing, and that has not made them Gautam Buddhas.

If you want to understand exactly what meditation is, Gautam Buddha is the first man to come to its right, exact definition – that is witnessing. [6]

YOU CAN NEVER go beyond the mind if you go on using it. You have to take a jump, and meditation means that jump. That's why meditation is illogical, irrational. And it cannot be made logical; it cannot be re- *meditation is* A JUMP duced to reason. You have to experience it. If you experience, only then do you know.

So try this: don't think about it, try – try to be a witness to your own thoughts. Sit down, relaxed, close your eyes, let your thoughts run just like pictures run on a screen. See them, look at them, make them your objects. One thought arises: look at it deeply. Don't think about it, just look at it. If you begin to think about it then you are not a witness – you have fallen in the trap.

There is a horn outside; a thought arises, 'some car is passing'; or a dog barks, or something happens. Don't think about it; just look at the thought. The thought has arisen, taken form. Now it is before you. Soon it will pass. Another thought will replace it. Go on looking at this thought process. Even for a single moment, if you are capable of looking at this thought process without thinking about it, you will have gained something in witnessing and you will have known something in witnessing. This is a taste, a different taste than thinking – totally different. But one has to experiment with it. Religion and science are poles apart, but in one thing they are similar and their emphasis is the same: science depends on experiment, and religion also. Only philosophy is non-experimental. Philosophy depends just on thinking. Religion and science both depend on experiment: science on objects, religion on your subjectivity. Science depends on experimenting with other things than you, and religion depends on experimenting directly with you.

It is difficult, because in science the experimenter is there, the experiment is there and the object to be experimented upon is there. There are three things: the object, the subject and the experiment. In religion you are all the three simultaneously. You are to experiment upon yourself. You are the subject and you are the object and you are the lab. Don't go on thinking. Begin, start somewhere, to experiment. Then you will have a direct feeling of what thinking is and what witnessing is. And then you will come to know that you cannot do both simultaneously, just as you cannot run and sit simultaneously. If you run, then you cannot sit, then you are not sitting. And if you are sitting, then you cannot run. But sitting is not a function of the legs. Running is a function of the legs; sitting is not a function of legs. Rather, sitting is a non-function of the legs. When the legs are functioning, then you are not sitting. Sitting is a non-function of the legs; running is the function.

The same is with the mind: thinking is a function of the mind; witnessing a non-function of the mind. When the mind is not functioning, you have the witnessing, then you have the awareness. [7]

MEDITATION IS A pure, scientific method. In science you call it observation, observation of the objects. When you move inwards it is the

meditation is SCIENTIFIC

same observation just taking a one-hundred-and-eighty-degree turn and looking in. That's what we call meditation. No god is needed, no Bible is needed. You need not have a belief system as a prerequisite.

An atheist can meditate, just as anybody else can, because meditation is only a method of turning inwards. [8]

YOU DON'T BELIEVE in God? That is not a hindrance to meditation. You don't believe in soul? That is not a hindrance in meditation. You don't believe at all? That is not an *meditation is* AN EXPERIMENT obstacle. You can meditate, because meditation simply says how to go withinwards: whether there is a soul or not doesn't matter; whether there is a God or not doesn't matter.

One thing is certain, that you are. Whether you will be after death, or not, does not matter. Only one thing matters: right this moment, you are. Who are you? To enter into it is meditation: to go deeper into your own being. Maybe it is just momentary; maybe you are not eternal; maybe death finishes everything. We don't make any condition that you have to believe. We say only that you have to experiment. Just try. One day it happens: thoughts are not there. And suddenly, when thoughts disappear, the body and you are separate – because thoughts are the bridge. Through thoughts you are joined with the body; it is the link. Suddenly the link disappears – you are there, the body is there, and there is an infinite abyss between the two. Then you know that the body will die, but you cannot die.

Then it is not something like a dogma; it is not a creed, it is an experience – self-evident. On that day, death disappears; on that day, doubt disappears, because now you are not always having to defend yourself. Nobody can destroy you, you are indestructible. Then trust arises, overflows. And to be in trust is to be in ecstasy; to be in trust is to be in god; to be in trust is to be fulfilled.

So I don't say cultivate trust. I say experiment with meditation. [9]

MIND MEANS WORDS; self means silence. Mind is nothing but all the words that you have accumulated; silence is that which has always *meditation is* SILENCE been with you, it is not an accumulation. That is the meaning of self. It is your intrinsic quality. On the background of silence you go on accumulating words, and the words in total are known as the mind. Silence is meditation. It is a question of changing the gestalt, shifting the attention from words into silence – which is always there.[10]

MEDITATION IS A natural state – which we have lost. It is a paradise lost, but the paradise can be regained. Look into the child's eyes... look and you will see tremendous silence, innocence. Each *meditation is* PARADISE child comes with a meditative state, but he has to be initiated into the ways of the society – he has to be taught how to think, how to calculate, how to reason, how to argue; he has to be taught words, language, concepts. And, slowly slowly, he loses contact with his own innocence. He becomes contaminated, polluted by the society. He becomes an efficient mechanism; he is no more a man.

All that is needed is to regain that space once more. You had known it before, so when for the first time you know meditation, you will be surprised – because a great feeling will arise in you as if you have known it before. And that feeling is true: you have known it before. You have forgotten. The diamond is lost in piles of rubbish. But if you can uncover it, you will find the diamond again – it is yours.

It cannot really be lost: it can only be forgotten. We are born as meditators, then we learn the ways of the mind. But our real nature remains hidden somewhere deep down like an undercurrent. Any day, a little digging, and you will find the source still flowing, the source of fresh waters. And the greatest joy in life is to find it.[11]

WHEREVER YOU ARE, remember yourself, that you are; this consciousness that you are should become a continuity. Not your name, your caste, your nationality – those *meditation is* REMEMBRANCE are futile things, absolutely useless. Just remember that 'I am'. This must not be forgotten. This is what Hindus call self-remembrance, what the Buddha called right-mindfulness, what Gurdjieff used to call self-remembering, what Krishnamurti calls awareness.

This is the most substantial part of meditation, to remember that 'I am'. Walking, sitting, eating, talking, remember that 'I am'. Never forget this. It will be difficult, very arduous. In the beginning you will keep forgetting; there will be only single moments when you will feel illumin-ated, then it is lost. But don't get miserable; even single moments are much. Go on, whenever you can remember again, again catch hold of the thread. When you forget, don't worry – remember again, again catch hold of the thread, and by and by the gaps will lessen, the intervals will start dropping, a continuity will arise. And whenever your consciousness becomes continuous, you need not use the mind. Then there is no planning, then you act out of your consciousness, not out of your mind. Then there is no need for any apology, no need to give any explanation. Then you are whatsoever you are, there is nothing to hide. Whatsoever you are, you are. You cannot do anything else. You can only be in a state of continuous remembrance. Through this remembrance, this mindfulness, comes the authentic religion, comes the authentic morality.[12]

IF LIFE GOES naturally, beautifully, if there are no life-negative teachers, if there are no politicians and priests to distract you – then nearabout the age of forty-two, exactly *meditation is* FREEDOM as sexual maturity comes, comes meditation maturity. Nearabout the age of forty-two, one starts feeling to fall withinwards. Near the age of fourteen, one starts falling towards the other, becomes extrovert. Love is extroversion; relationship is to think of the other. Meditation is introversion; meditation is to think of one's own self, of one's own center.

Between the age of fourteen and the age of forty-two there comes a change. By and by one lives life, knows what love is, knows its fulfillment and its frustration, knows its joy and its sadness, knows its beauty and its ugliness, knows that there are moments of great ecstasy and then great valleys of darkness. Then one starts by and by moving towards his own self, because to depend on the other can never be really ecstatic. If your joy depends on the other, that joy can never have the quality of freedom in it. And a joy which does not have the quality of freedom is not much joy. If you are dependent on the other, then there is a limitation. The joy that comes through love is momentary. You can meet with the other only for moments, and then again you are separate and you fall apart. Just in the middle of it you fall apart. Just for a moment you become joined together. Then one starts thinking, 'Is there a way to become one with existence and never to fall apart again?'

That's what meditation is. Love is joining with existence through another person for only moments. Meditation is getting joined together with existence eternally.

'Yoga' means 'to join together.' This has to happen somewhere in the deepest core. And then there is joy and then there is freedom. And then there is bliss and there is no dark valley following it. Then happiness is eternal, then celebration is eternal [13]

IT IS THE light of awareness that makes things precious, extraordinary. Then small things are no longer small. When a man with alert-
meditation is SENSITIVITY ness, sensitivity, love, touches an ordinary pebble on the seashore, that pebble becomes a

Kohinoor. And if you touch a Kohinoor in your unconscious state, it is just an ordinary pebble – not even that. Your life will have as much depth and as much meaning as you have awareness.

Now people are asking all over the world, "What is the meaning of life?" Of course the meaning is lost, because you have lost the way to find the meaning – and the way is awareness.[14]

GROWING OLD IS not of any worth, every animal does it, it needs no intelligence. Growing up is a totally different experience. Growing old is horizontal; growing up is vertical, it leads *meditation is* GROWING UP you to heights, it leads you to depths.

And strangely enough, you will be surprised to know that time is horizontal. One moment passes, another moment comes, another moment, another moment... in a line, a horizontal line. Time is horizontal, and mind is also horizontal. One thought is followed by another thought, and by another thought, and by another thought, but in a line, in a row, a procession, or just a traffic – but it is going horizontal.

Meditation is vertical, it is going beyond mind and beyond time. And perhaps, ultimately you will find that time and mind are equivalent, two names of the same phenomenon – the horizontal procession of thoughts, of moments. Meditation is to stop time and mind both, and suddenly you start rising up in eternity. Eternity is not part of time, and eternity is not a thought; it is an experience.[15]

THE MAN WHO lives in the future, lives a counterfeit life. He does not really live, he only pretends to live. He hopes to live, he desires to live, but he never lives.

meditation is NOT ESCAPIST

And the tomorrow never comes, it is always today. And whatsoever comes is always now and here, and he does not know how to live now-here; he knows only how to escape from now-here. The way to escape is called "desire," *tanha* – that is Buddha's word for what is an escape from the present, from the real into the unreal.

The man who desires is an escapist.

Now, this is very strange, that meditators are thought to be escapists. That is utter nonsense. Only the meditator is not an escapist – everybody else is. Meditation means getting out of desire, getting out of thoughts, getting out of mind. Meditation means relaxing in the moment, in the present. Meditation is the only thing in the world which is not escapist, although it is thought to be the most escapist thing. People who condemn meditation always condemn it with the argument that it is escape, escaping from life. They are simply talking nonsense; they don't understand what they are saying.

Meditation is not escaping from life: it is escaping into life. Mind is escaping from life, desire is escaping from life.[16]

IT IS THE simplest art in the world, to be silent. It is not a doing, it is a non-doing. How can it be difficult?

***meditation is* A KNACK** I am showing you the way of enlightenment through laziness! Nothing has to be done to attain it, because it is your nature. You have already got it. You are just so busy with outer business that you cannot see your own nature.

Deep within you is exactly the same as outside you: the beauty, the silence, the ecstasy, the blissfulness. But please, sometimes be kind to yourself: just sit down and don't do anything, either physically or mentally. Relax, not in an American way... because I have seen so many American books titled *How to Relax*. The very title says that the man knows nothing about relaxation. There is no "how."

Yes, it is okay – *How to Repair a Car;* you will have to do something. But there is no doing as such, as far as relaxation is concerned. Just don't do anything. I know you will find it a little difficult in the beginning. That is not because relaxation is difficult, it is because you have become addicted to doing something. That addiction will take a little time to disappear.

Just be, and watch. Being is not doing, and watching is also not doing. You sit silently doing nothing, witnessing whatsoever is happening. Thoughts will be moving in your mind; your body may be feeling some tension somewhere, you may have a migraine. Just be a witness. Don't be identified with it. Watch, be a watcher on the hills, and everything else is happening in the valley. It is a knack, not an art.

Meditation is not a science, it is not an art, it is a knack – just that way. All that you need is a little patience.

The old habits will continue; the thoughts will go on rushing. And your mind is always in a rush hour, the traffic is always jammed. Your body is not accustomed to sitting silently – you will be tossing and turning. Nothing to be worried about. Just watch that the body is tossing and turning, that the mind is whirling, is full of thoughts – consistent, inconsistent, useless – fantasies, dreams. You remain in the center, just watching.

All the religions of the world have taught people to do something: stop the process of thought, force the body into a still posture. That's what yoga is – a long practice of forcing the body to be still. But a forced body is not still. And all the prayers, concentrations, contemplations of all the religions do the same with the mind: they force it, they don't allow the thoughts to move. Yes, you have the capacity to do it. And if you persist you may be able to stop the thought process. But this is not the real thing, it is absolutely fake.

When stillness comes on its own, when silence descends without your effort, when you watch thoughts and a moment comes when thoughts start disappearing and silence starts happening, that is beautiful. The thoughts stop of their own accord if you don't identify, if you remain a witness and you don't say, "This is my thought."

You don't say, "This is bad, this is good," "This should be there" and "This should not be there" Then you are not a watcher; you have prejudices, you have certain attitudes. A watcher has no prejudice, he has no judgment. He simply sees like a mirror.

When you bring something in front of a mirror it reflects, simply reflects. There is no judgment that the man is ugly, that the man is beautiful, that, "Aha! What a good nose you have got." The mirror has nothing to say. Its nature is to mirror; it mirrors. This is what I call meditation: you simply mirror everything within or without.

And I guarantee you.... I can guarantee because it has happened to me and to many of my people; just watching patiently – maybe a few days will pass, maybe a few months, maybe a few years. There is no way of saying because each individual has a different collection.

You must have seen people collecting antiques, postal stamps. Everybody has a different collection; the quantity may be different, hence the time it takes will be different – but go on remaining a witness as much as you can. And this meditation needs no special time. You can wash the floor and remain silently watching yourself washing the floor.

I can move my hand unconsciously, without watching, or I can move it with full awareness. And there is a qualitative difference. When you move it unconsciously it is mechanical. When you move it with consciousness there is grace. Even in the hand, which is part of your body, you will feel silence, coolness – what to say about the mind?

With your watching and watching, slowly the rush of thoughts starts getting less and less. Moments of silence start appearing; a thought comes, and then there is silence before another thought appears. These gaps will give you the first glimpse of meditation and the first joy that you are arriving home.[17]

ONCE YOU UNDERSTAND what meditation is things become very clear. Otherwise, you can go on groping in the dark.

Meditation is a state of clarity, not a state of mind. *meditation is* CLARITY
Mind is confusion. Mind is never clear. It cannot be. Thoughts create clouds around you – they are subtle clouds. A mist is created by them, and the clarity is lost. When thoughts disappear, when there are no more clouds around you, when you are in your simple beingness, clarity happens. Then you can see far away; then you can see to the very end of existence; then your gaze becomes penetrating – to the very core of being.

Meditation is clarity, absolute clarity, of vision. You cannot think about it. You have to drop thinking.[18]

35

FOR CENTURIES EMPTINESS has been condemned. Emptiness is beautiful. And the foolish people have been telling you, "The empty mind is the devil's workshop." The

meditation is EMPTINESS

empty mind is God's workshop! The occupied mind is the devil's workshop.

But one has to be truly empty. Just being lazy does not mean that you are empty; not doing anything does not mean that you are empty. Thousands of thoughts are clamoring inside. You may be lazy on the outside, but inside much work is going on. Many walls are being created, new prisons are being prepared, so that when you get fed up with the old you can enter into the new. Old chains may break any time so you are creating new chains in case the old chains break; then you will feel very empty.

Once in a while it happens naturally – because it is your very nature to be free. So once in a while, in spite of you... seeing a sunset, suddenly you forget all your desires. You forget all lust, all hankering for pleasure. The sunset is so beautiful, so overwhelming, that you forget the past and the future; only the present remains. You are so one with the moment, there is no observer and no observed. The observer becomes the observed. You are not separate from the sunset.

You are bridged; in such a communion you come into a clearing, and because of the clearing you feel joyous. But again you are back into the black hole for the simple reason that coming out into the clearing you need courage to remain in the empty sky.

That's what I call *sannyas*.

This courage I call *sannyas* – not escaping but coming into the clearing, seeing the sky unclouded, listening to the songs of the birds without distorting. And then again and again you are becoming more and more attuned with the emptiness and the joy of being empty. Slowly slowly, you see that emptiness is not just empti-ness; it is fullness, but a fullness of which you have never been aware, a fullness of which you have never tasted.

So in the beginning it looks empty; in the end it is

full, totally full, overflowingly full. It is full of peace, it is full of silence, it is full of light.[19]

HAVE A VERY penetrating eye inside your mind – see what its motivations are. When you do something, immediately look for the motivation, *meditation is* INTELLIGENCE because if you miss the motivation, the mind goes on befooling you and goes on saying that something else was the motivation. For example: you come home angry and you beat your child. The mind will say, 'It is just for his own sake, to make him behave.' This is a rationalization. Go deeper... You were angry and you wanted somebody with whom you could be angry. You could not be angry with the boss in the office, he is too strong for that. And it is risky and econ-omically dangerous. No, you needed somebody helpless. Now this child is perfectly helpless, he

38

depends on you; he cannot react, he cannot do anything, he cannot pay you back in the same coin. You cannot find a more perfect victim.

Look. Are you angry with the child? If you are, then the mind is befooling you.

The mind goes on befooling you twenty-four hours a day and you cooperate with it. Then in the end you are in misery, you land in hell. Watch every moment for the right motivation. If you can find the right motivation, the mind will become more and more incapable of deceiving you. And the further away you are from deception, the more you will be capable of moving beyond mind, the more you will become a master.

I have heard....

One scientist was saying to his friend, "I don't see why you insisted that your wife wear a chastity belt while we were away at the convention. After all, between us as old buddies, with Emma's face and figure, who would...?"

"I know, I know," replied the other. "But when I get back home, I can always say I lost the key."

Look, watch for the unconscious motivation. The

mind goes on bullying you and bossing you because you are not capable of seeing its real motivations. Once a person becomes capable of seeing real motivations, meditation is very close... because then the mind no longer has a grip on you.

The mind is a mechanism, it has no intelligence. The mind is a biocomputer – how can it have any intelligence? It has skill, but it has no intelligence; it has a functional utility, but it has no awareness. It is a robot; it works well but don't listen to it too much because then you will lose your inner intelligence. Then it is as if you are asking a machine to guide you, lead you. You are asking a machine which has nothing original in it – cannot have. Not a single thought in the mind is ever original, it is always a repetition. Watch: whenever mind says something, see that it is again putting you into a routine. Try to do something new and the mind will have less grip on you.

People who are in some way creative are always easily transformed into meditators, and people who are uncreative in their life are the most difficult. If you live a repetitive life the mind has too much control over you – you cannot move away from it, you are afraid. Do something new every day. Don't listen to the old routine. In fact, if the mind says something, tell it, "This we have been doing always. Now let us do something else." Even small changes... in the way you have always been behaving with your wife – just small changes; in the way you always walk – just small changes; the way you always talk – small changes. And you will find that the mind is losing its grip on you, you are becoming a little freer.[20]

WHATSOEVER YOU DO, do it with deep alertness; then even small things become sacred. Then cooking or cleaning become sacred; they become worship. It is not a question of what you *meditation is* CLEANSING are doing, the question is how you are doing it. You can clean the floor like a robot, a mechanical thing; you have to clean it, so you clean it. Then you miss something beautiful. Then you waste those moments in only cleaning the floor. Cleaning the floor could have been a great experience; you missed it. The floor is cleaned but something that could have happened within you has not happened. If you were aware, not only the floor but you would have felt a deep cleansing. Clean the floor full of awareness, luminous with awareness. Work or sit or walk, but one thing has to be a continuous thread: make more and more moments of your life luminous with awareness. Let the candle of awareness burn in each moment, in each act. The cumulative effect is what enlightenment is. The cumulative effect, all the moments together, all small candles together, become a great source of light.[21]

REMEMBER MEDITATION WILL bring you more and more intelligence, infinite intelligence, a radiant intelligence. Meditation will make you more alive and sensitive; your life *meditation is* A FLOWERING will become richer. Look at the ascetics: their life has become almost as if it is not life. These people are not meditators. They may be masochists, torturing themselves and enjoying the torture...

The mind is very cunning, it goes on doing things and rationalizing them. Ordinarily you are violent towards others but mind is very cunning – it can learn non violence, it can preach nonviolence. then it becomes violent towards itself. And the violence that you do on your own self is respected by people because they have an idea that to be an ascetic is to be religious. That is sheer nonsense.

God is not an ascetic, otherwise there would be no flowers, there would be no green trees, only deserts. God is not an ascetic, otherwise there would be no song in life, no dance in life – only cemeteries and cemeteries. God is not an ascetic; God enjoys life. God is more Epicurean than you can imagine. If you think about God, think in terms of Epicurus. God is a constant search for more and more happiness, joy, ecstasy. Remember that.

But mind is very cunning. It can rationalize paralysis as meditation; it can rationalize dullness as transcendence; it can rationalize deadness as renunciation. Watch out. Always remember that if you are moving in the right direction you will go on flowering.[22]

AND REMEMBER, EACH situation has to become an opportunity to meditate. What is meditation? Becoming aware of what you are doing, becom-

meditation is AWARENESS

ing aware of what is happening to you.

Somebody insults you: become aware. What is happening to you when the insult reaches you? Meditate over it; this is changing the whole gestalt. When somebody insults you, you concentrate on the person – 'Why is he insulting me? Who does he think he is? How can I take revenge?' If he is very powerful you surrender, you start wagging your tail. If he is not very powerful and you see that he is weak, you pounce on him. But you forget yourself completely in all this; the other becomes the focus. This is missing an opportunity for meditation. When somebody insults you, meditate.

Gurdjieff has said, "When my father was dying, I was only nine. He called me close to his bed and whispered in my ear, 'My son, I am not leaving much to you, not in worldly things, but I have one thing to tell you that was told to me by my father on his deathbed. It has helped me tremendously; it has been my treasure. You are not very grown up yet, you may not understand what I am saying, but keep it, remember it. One day you will be grown up and then you may understand. This is a key: it unlocks the doors of great treasures.'"

Of course Gurdjieff could not understand it at that moment, but it was the thing that changed his whole life. And his father said a very simple thing. He said, "Whenever somebody insults you, my son, tell him you will meditate over it for twenty-four hours and then you will come and answer him."

Gurdjieff could not believe that this was such a great key. He could not believe that 'This is something so valuable that I have to remember it.' And we can forgive a young child of nine years old. But because this was something said by his dying father who had loved him tremendously, and immediately after saying it he breathed his last, it became imprinted on him; he could not forget it. Whenever he remembered his father, he would remember the saying.

Without truly understanding, he started practicing it. If somebody insulted him he would say, "Sir, for twenty-four hours I have to meditate over it – that's what my father told me. And he is here no more, and I cannot disobey a dead old man. He loved me tremendously, and I loved him tremendously, and now there is no way to disobey him. You can disobey your father when he is alive, but when your father is dead how can you disobey him? So please forgive me, I will come back after twenty-four hours and answer you." And he says, "Meditating on it for twenty-four hours has given me the greatest insights into my being. Sometimes I found that the insult was right, that that's how I am. So I would go to the person and say, 'Sir, thank you, you were right. It was not an insult, it was simply a statement of fact. You called me stupid; I am.'

"Or sometimes it happened that meditating for twenty-four hours, I would come to know that it was an absolute lie. But when something is a lie, why be offended by it? So I would not even go to tell him that it was a lie. A lie is a lie, why be bothered by it?"

But watching, meditating, slowly slowly he became more and more aware of his reactions, rather than the actions of others.[23]

MILLIONS OF PEOPLE miss meditation because meditation has taken on a wrong connotation. It looks very serious, looks gloomy, has something of *meditation is* FUN the church in it, looks as if it is only for people who are dead, or almost dead, who are gloomy, serious, have long faces, who have lost festivity, fun, playfulness, celebration. These are the qualities of meditation. A really meditative person is playful: life is fun for him, life is a *leela*, a play. He enjoys it tremendously. He is not serious. He is relaxed.[24]

YOU WILL HAVE to understand one of the most fundamental things about meditation – that no technique leads to meditation.

meditation is UNDERSTANDING The old so-called tech-niques and the new scientific bio-feedback tech-niques are the same as far as meditation is concerned.

Meditation is not a byproduct of any technique.

Meditation happens beyond mind. No technique can go beyond mind.

But there is going to be a great misunderstanding in scientific circles, and it has a certain basis. The basis of all misunderstanding is: When the being of a person is in a state of meditation, it creates certain waves in the mind. These waves can be created from the outside by technical means. But those waves will not create meditation – this is the misunderstanding.

Meditation creates those waves; it is the mind reflecting the inner world.

You cannot see what is happening inside. But you can see what is happening in the mind. Now there are sensitive instruments... we can judge what kind of waves are there when a person is asleep, what kinds of waves are there when a person is dreaming, what kinds of waves are there when a person is in meditation.

But by creating the waves, you cannot create the situation – because those waves are only symptoms, indicators.

It is perfectly good, you can study them. But remember that there is no shortcut to meditation, and no mechanical device can be of any help. In fact, meditation needs no technique – scientific or otherwise.

Meditation is simply an understanding.

It is not a question of sitting silently, it is not a question of chanting a mantra. It is a question of understanding the subtle workings of the mind. As you understand those workings of the mind a great awareness arises in you which is not of the mind. That awareness arises in your being, in your soul, in your consciousness.

Mind is only a mechanism, but when that awareness arises it is bound to create a certain energy pattern around it. That energy pattern is noted by the mind. Mind is a very subtle mechanism.

And you are studying from the outside, so at the most you can study the mind. Seeing that whenever a person is silent, serene, peaceful, a certain wave pattern always, inevitably appears in the mind, the scientific thinking will say: if we can create this wave pattern in the mind, through some biofeedback technology, then the being inside will reach the heights of awareness.

This is not going to happen.

It is not a question of cause and effect.

These waves in the mind are not the cause of meditation; they are, on the contrary, the effect. But from the effect you cannot move towards the cause. It is possible that by biofeedback you can create certain patterns in the mind and they will give a feeling of peace, silence and serenity to the person. Because the person himself does not know what meditation is and has no way of comparing, he may be misled into believing that this is meditation – but it is not. Because the moment the biofeedback mechanism stops, the waves disappear, and the silence and the peace and the serenity also disappear.

And you may go on practicing with those scientific instruments for years; it will not change your character, it will not change your morality, it will not change your individuality. You will remain the same.

Meditation transforms. It takes you to higher levels of consciousness and changes your whole lifestyle. It changes your reactions into responses to such an extent that it is unbelievable that the person who would have reacted in the same situation in anger is now acting in deep compassion, with love – in the same situation.

Meditation is a state of being, arrived at through understanding.

It needs intelligence, it does not need techniques.[25]

MEDITATION IS JUST being delighted in your own presence; meditation is a delight in your own being. It is very simple – a totally relaxed state of

meditation is DELIGHT

consciousness where you are not doing anything. The moment doing enters, you become tense; anxiety enters immediately. How to do? What to do? How to succeed? How not to fail? You have already moved into the future. Meditation is just to be, not doing anything – no action, no thought, no emotion. You just are, and it is a sheer delight.

From where does this delight come when you are not doing anything? It comes from nowhere, or, it comes from everywhere. It is uncaused, because the existence is made of the stuff called joy. It needs no cause, no reason. If you are unhappy you have a reason to be unhappy; if you are happy you are simply happy – there is no reason for it. Your mind tries to find a reason because it cannot believe in the uncaused because it can not control the uncaused – with the uncaused the mind simply becomes impotent. So the mind goes on finding some reason or other. But I would like to tell you that whenever you are happy, you are happy for no reason at all. Whenever you are unhappy, you have some reason to be unhappy – because happiness is just the stuff you are made of. It is your very being, it is your innermost core. Joy is your innermost core.

Look at the trees, look at the birds, look at the

clouds, look at the stars... and if you have eyes you will be able to see that the whole existence is joyful. Everything is simply happy. Trees are happy for no reason; they are not going to become prime ministers or presidents and they are not going to become rich and they will never have any bank balance. Look at the flowers – for no reason. It is simply unbelievable how happy flowers are.

The whole existence is made of the stuff called joy.[26]

MEDITATION IS REST, absolute rest, a full stop to all activity – physical, mental, emotional. When you are in such a deep rest that nothing stirs in you,

meditation is RELAXATION when all action as such ceases, as if you are fast asleep yet awake, you come to know who you are. Suddenly the window opens. It cannot be opened by effort, because effort creates tension and tension is the cause of our whole misery. Hence this is something very fundamental to be understood, that meditation is not effort.

One has to be very playful about meditation, one has to learn to enjoy it as fun. One has not to be serious about it – be serious and you miss. One has to go into it very joyously. And one has to keep aware that it is falling into deeper and deeper rest. It is not concentration; just the contrary, it is relaxation. When you are utterly relaxed, for the first time you start feeling your reality; you come face to face with your being. When you are engaged in activity you are so occupied that you cannot see yourself. Activity creates much smoke around you, it raises much dust around you; hence all activity has to be dropped, at least for a few hours every day.

That is only so in the beginning. When you have learned the art of being at rest then you can be both active and restful together, because then you know that rest is something so inner that it cannot be disturbed by anything outer. The activity goes on at the circumference and at the center you remain restful. So it is only for beginning that activity has to be dropped for a few hours. When one has learned the art then there is no question: for twenty-four hours a day one can be meditative and one can continue all the activities of ordinary life.

But remember, the key word is rest, relaxation. Never go against rest and relaxation. Arrange your life in such a way, drop all futile activity, because ninety per cent is futile; it is just for killing time and remaining occupied. Do only the essential and devote your energies more and more to the inner journey. Then that miracle happens when you can remain at rest and in action together, simultaneously. That is the meeting of the sacred and the mundane, the meeting of this world and that, the meeting of materialism and spiritualism.[27]

IF YOU GO to Catholic, Jaina, Buddhist monks, you will find them very nervous – maybe not so nervous in their monasteries, but if you bring them out to the world, you will find them very, very *meditation is* COOL nervous because on each step there is temptation. A man of meditation comes to a point where there is no temptation left. Try to understand it. Temptation never comes from without; it is the repressed desire, repressed energy, repressed anger, repressed sex, repressed greed, that creates temptation. Temptation comes from within you, it has nothing to do with the without. It is not that a devil comes and tempts you, it is your own repressed mind that becomes devilish and wants to take revenge. To control that mind one has to remain so cold and frozen that no life energy is allowed to move into your limbs, into your body. If energy is allowed to move, those repressions will surface. That's why people have learned how to be cold, how to touch others and yet not touch them, how to see people and yet not see them. People live with clichès – 'Hello, how are you?' Nobody means anything. These are just to avoid the real encounter of two persons. People don't look into each other's eyes, they don't hold hands, they don't try to feel each other's energy, they don't allow each other to pour. Very afraid, somehow just managing...cold and dead, in a strait-jacket.

A man of meditation has learned how to be full of energy, at the maximum, optimum. He lives at the peak, he makes his abode at the peak. Certainly he has a warmth but it is not feverish, it only shows life. He is not hot, he is cool, because he is not carried away by desires. He is so happy, that he is no longer seeking any happiness. He is so at ease, he is so at home, he is not going anywhere, he is not running and chasing... he is very cool.[28]

SEX HAS SO much appeal because in sex you become one for a moment. But in that moment, you are unconscious. You seek the unconsciousness because you seek the oneness. But the more you

meditation is ONENESS

seek it, the more conscious you become. Then you will not feel the bliss of sex, because the bliss was coming from the unconsciousness.

You could become unconscious in a moment of passion. Your consciousness dropped. For a single moment you were in the abyss – but unconscious. But the more you seek it, the more it is lost. Finally a moment comes when you are in sex and the moment of unconsciousness no longer happens. The abyss is lost, the bliss is lost. Then the act becomes stupid. It is just a mechanical release; there is nothing spiritual about it.

We have known only unconscious oneness; we have never known conscious oneness. Meditation is conscious oneness. It is the other pole of sexuality. Sex is one pole, unconscious oneness; meditation is the other pole, conscious oneness. Sex is the lowest point of oneness and meditation is the peak, the highest peak of oneness. The difference is a difference of consciousness.

The Western mind is thinking about meditation now because the appeal of sex has been lost. Whenever a society becomes nonsuppressive sexually, meditation will follow, because uninhibited sex will kill the charm and romance of sex; it will kill the spiritual side of it. Much sex is there, but you cannot continue to be unconscious in it.

A sexually suppressed society can remain sexual, but a nonsuppressive, uninhibited society cannot remain with sexuality forever. It will have to be transcended. So if a society is sexual, meditation will follow. To me, a sexually free society is the first step toward seeking, searching.[29]

I AM NOT against sex, and I am not saying drop sex. I am saying understand it, meditate over it – don't just go on making love in an unconscious way – and that will

meditation is RECREATION

become your greatest meditation. Be more conscious, alert, aware, and see what is actually happening. Is this moment of bliss coming through sex or because there is no sex any more for a few moments and the desire has disappeared? For a few hours after sex you don't think of sex, hence the peace, the calm, the quiet. Again the desire will come and again the desire will disturb; again there will be turmoil and the lake will have ripples, waves.

If one meditates on one's sexuality, one starts understanding great secrets of life; they are hidden there. Sex is holding the very key. It is not only the key to reproduce children, it is also the key to recreate yourself again. It is not only reproduction, it is really recreation.

In English the word 'recreation' has lost its original meaning. Now 'recreation' means enjoying a holiday, enjoying fun, playing around. But in fact, whenever you are playing and you are on a holiday, something is created in you – it is actually recreation, it is not just fun. Something that dies in work and in the day-to-day world, is born again. And sex has become the most recreational act in people's lives. That is their recreation. But on a higher plane it is really recreation, it is not just fun. It holds great secrets in it, and the first secret is – if you meditate you will see it – that joy comes because sex disappears. And whenever you are in that moment of joy, time also disappears – if you meditate on it – the mind also disappears. And these are the qualities of meditation.

My own observation is that the first glimpse of meditation in the world must have come through sex; there is no other way. Meditation must have entered into life through sex, because this is the most meditative phenomenon – if you understand it, if you go deep into it, if you just don't use it like a drug. Then slowly slowly as more understanding grows, the more the hankering disappears, and one day comes of great freedom when sex no more haunts you. Then one is quiet, silent, utterly oneself. The need for the other has disappeared. One can still make love if one chooses to, but there is no need.

Then it will be a kind of sharing.[30]

WHEN I SAY, "Drop the ego, drop the mind," I don't mean that you cannot use the mind any more. In fact, when you don't cling to the mind you can use it in a far better, far *meditation is* REST more efficient way, because the energy that was involved in clinging becomes available. And when you are not continuously in the mind, twenty-four hours a day in the mind, the mind also gets a little time to rest.

Do you know? – even metals need rest, even metals get tired. So what to say about this subtle mechanism of the mind? It is the most subtle mechanism in the world. In such a small skull you are carrying such a complicated biocomputer that no computer made by man is yet capable of competing with it. The scientists say a single man's brain can contain all the libraries of the world and yet there will be space enough to contain more.

And you are continuously using it – uselessly, unnecessarily! You have forgotten how to put it off. For seventy, eighty years it remains on, working, working, tired. That's why people lose intelligence: for the simple reason that they are so tired. If the mind can have a little rest, if you can leave the mind alone for a few hours every day, if once in a while you can give the mind a holiday, it will be rejuvenated; it will come out more intelligent, more efficient, more skillful.

So I am not saying that you are not to use your mind, but don't be used by the mind. Right now the mind is the master and you are only a slave.

Meditation makes you a master and the mind becomes a slave. And remember: the mind as a master is dangerous because, after all, it is a machine; but the mind as a slave is tremendously significant, useful. A machine should function as a machine, not as a master. Our priorities are all upside-down – your consciousness should be the master.

So whenever you want to use it, in the East or in the West – of course you will need it in the marketplace – use it! But when you don't need it, when you are resting at home by the side of your swimming pool or in your garden, there is no need. Put it aside. Forget all about it! Then just be.[31]

SOCIETY CANNOT EXIST without language; it needs language. But existence does not need it. I am not saying that you should exist without language. You will have to *meditation is* MASTERY use it. But you must be able to turn the mechanism of verbalization on and off. When you are existing as a social being, the mechanism of language is needed; but when you are alone with existence, you must be able to turn it off. If you can't turn it off – if it goes on and on, and you are incapable of stopping it – then you have become a slave to it. Mind must be an instrument, not the master.

When mind is the master, a non-meditative state exists. When you are the master, your consciousness is the master, a meditative state exists. So meditation means becoming a master of the mechanism of the mind.[32]

BE AWARE OF your mental processes, how your mind works. The moment you become aware of the functioning of your mind, you are not *meditation is* IN THE GAP the mind. The very awareness means that you are beyond: aloof, a witness. And the more aware you become, the more you will be able to see the gaps between the experience and the words. Gaps are there, but you are so unaware that they are never seen.

Between two words there is always a gap, however imperceptible, however small. Otherwise the two words cannot remain two; they will become one. Between two notes of music there is always a gap, a silence. Two words or two notes cannot be two unless there is an interval between them. A silence is always there but one has to be really aware, really attentive, to feel it.

The more aware you become, the slower the mind becomes. It is always relative. The less aware you are, the faster the mind is; the more aware you are, the slower the process of the mind is. When you are more aware of the mind, the mind slows down and the gaps between thoughts widen. Then you can see them.

It is just like a film. When a projector is run in slow motion, you see the gaps. If I raise my hand, this has to be shot in a thousand parts. Each part will be a single photograph. If these thousands of single photographs pass before your eyes so fast that you cannot see the gaps, then you see the hand raised as a process. But in slow motion, the gaps can be seen.

Mind is just like a film. Gaps are there. The more attentive you are to your mind, the more you will see them. It is just like a gestalt picture: a picture that contains two distinct images at the same time. One image can be seen or the other can be seen, but you cannot see both simultaneously. It can be a picture of an old lady, and at the same time a picture of a young lady. But if you are focused on one, you will not see the other; and when you are focused on the other, the first is lost. Even if you know perfectly well that you have seen both images, you cannot see them simultaneously.

The same thing happens with the mind. If you see the words you cannot see the gaps, and if you see the gaps you cannot see the words. Every word is followed by a gap and every gap is followed by a word, but you cannot see both simultaneously. If you are focused on the gaps, words will be lost and you will be thrown into meditation.

A consciousness that is focused only on words is non-meditative and a consciousness that is focused only on gaps is meditative. Whenever you become aware of the gaps, the words will be lost.

If you observe carefully, you will not find words; you will only find a gap.

You can feel the difference between two words, but you cannot feel the difference between two gaps. Words are always plural and the gap is always singular: "the" gap. They merge and become one. Meditation is a focusing on the gap.[33]

MIND CONCENTRATES: IT acts out of the past. Meditation acts in the present, out of the present. It is a pure response to the present, it is not reaction. It *meditation is* IN THE PRESENT acts not out of conclusions, it acts seeing the existential.

Watch in your life: there is a great difference when you act out of conclusions. You see a man, you feel attracted – a beautiful man, looks very good, looks innocent. His eyes are beautiful, the vibe is beautiful. But then the man introduces himself and he says, "I am a Jew" – and you are a Christian. Something immediately clicks and there is distance: now the man is no more innocent, the man is no more beautiful. You have certain ideas about Jews. Or, he is a Christian and you are a Jew; you have certain ideas about Christians – what Christianity has done to Jews in the past, what other Christians have done to Jews, how they have tortured Jews down the ages... and suddenly he is a Christian – and something immediately changes. This is acting out of conclusions, prejudices, not looking at this man – because this man may not be the man that you think a Jew has to be... because each Jew is a different kind of man, each Hindu is a different kind of man, so is each Mohammedan. You cannot act out of prejudices. You cannot act by categorizing people. You cannot pigeonhole people; nobody can be pigeonholed. You may have been deceived by a hundred communists, but when you meet the hundred and first communist don't go on believing in the category that you have made in your mind: that communists are deceptive – or anything. This may be a different type of man, because no two persons are alike. Whenever you act out of conclusions, it is mind. When you look into the present and you don't allow any idea to obstruct the reality, to obstruct the fact, you just look into the fact and act out of that look, that is meditation.[34]

WHEN I SAY, "You have to drop thinking," don't conclude in a hurry, because I have to use language. So I say, "Drop thinking," but if you start dropping, you will **meditation is** A HAPPENING miss, because again you will reduce it to a doing.

"Drop thinking" simply means: don't do anything. Sit. Let thoughts settle themselves. Let mind drop on its own accord. You just sit gazing at the wall, in a silent corner, not doing anything at all. Relaxed. Loose. With no effort. Not going anywhere. As if you are falling asleep awake – you are awake and you are relaxing but the whole body is falling into sleep. You remain alert inside but the whole body moves into deep relaxation.

Thoughts settle on their own accord, you need not jump amongst them, you need not try to put them right. It is as if a stream has become muddy... what do you do? Do you jump in it and start helping the stream to become clear? You will make it more muddy! You simply sit on the bank. You wait. There is nothing to be done, because whatsoever you do will make the stream more muddy. If somebody has passed through a stream and the dead leaves have surfaced and the mud has arisen, just patience is needed. You simply sit on the bank. Watch, indifferently. And as the stream goes on flowing, the dead leaves will be taken away, and the mud will start settling because it cannot hang forever. After a while, suddenly you will become aware – the stream is crystal-clear again.

Whenever a desire passes through your mind the stream becomes muddy. So just sit. Don't try to do anything. In Japan this 'just sitting' is called zazen; just sitting and doing nothing. And one day, meditation happens. Not that you bring it to you, it comes to you. And when it comes, you immediately recognize it; it has been always there but you were not looking in the right direction. The treasure has been with you but you were occupied somewhere else: in thoughts, in desires, in a thousand and one things. You were not interested in the only one thing... and that was your own being....

The more you understand the mechanism of the mind, the more the possibility is that you will not interfere. The more you understand how the mind functions, the more the possibility is that you will be able to sit in zazen. That you will be able just to sit, sit and do nothing, that you will be able to allow meditation to happen. It is a happening.[35]

IF YOU FEEL much resistance against meditation it simply shows that deep down you are alert that something is going to happen which will change

meditation is TRANSFORMATION

your whole life. You are afraid of being reborn. You have invested too much in your old habits, in the old personality, in the old identity.

Meditation is nothing but trying to clean your being, trying to become fresh and young, trying to become more alive and more alert. If you are afraid of meditation it means you are afraid of life, you are afraid of awareness, and the resistance comes because you know that if you move into meditation, something is bound to happen. If you are not resisting at all it may be because you don't take meditation very seriously, you don't take meditation very sincerely. Then you can play around; what is there to be afraid of? [36]

THERE ARE TWO planes in you: the plane of the mind, and the plane of the no-mind. Or, let me say it in this way: the plane when you are on the periphery of your being and *meditation is* COMING HOME the plane when you are at the center of your being. Every circle has a center – you may know it, you may not know it. You may not even suspect that there is a center, but there has to be. You are a periphery, you are a circle: there is a center. Without the center you cannot be; there is a nucleus of your being.

At that center you are already a buddha, a *siddha*, one who has already arrived home. On the periphery, you are in the world – in the mind, in dreams, in desires, in anxieties, in a thousand and one games. And you are both.

By and by, you will become capable of moving from the periphery to the center and from the center to the periphery very smoothly – just as you walk into your house and out of your house. You don't create any dichotomy. You don't say, "I am outside the house so how can I go inside the house?" You don't say, "I am inside the house so how can I come outside the house?" It is sunny outside, it is warm, pleasant – you sit outside in the garden. Then it is becoming hotter and hotter, and you start perspiring. Now it is no longer pleasant – it is becoming uncomfortable: you simply get up and move inside the house. There it is cool; there it is not uncomfortable. Now, there it is pleasant. You go on moving in and out.

In the same way a man of awareness and understanding moves from the periphery to the center, from the center to the periphery. He never gets fixated anywhere. From the marketplace to the monastery, from *sansar* to *sannyas*, from being extrovert to being introvert – he continuously goes on moving, because these two are his wings, they are not against each other. They may be balanced in opposite directions – they have to be; if both the wings are on one side, the bird cannot fly into the sky. They have to be balancing, they have to be in opposite directions, but still they belong to the same bird, and they serve the same bird. Your outside and your inside are your wings.

This has to be very deeply remembered, because there is a possibility... the mind tends to fixate. There are people who are fixated in the marketplace; they say they cannot get out of it; they say they have no time for meditation; they say even if time is there they don't know how to meditate and they don't believe that they can meditate. They say they are worldly – how can they meditate? They are materialistic – how can they meditate? They say, "Unfortunately, we are extroverts – how can we go in?"They have chosen only one wing. And, of course, if frustration comes out of it, it is natural. With one wing frustration is bound to come.

Then there are people who become fed up with the world and escape out of the world, go to the monasteries and the Himalayas, become sann-yasins, monks: start living alone, force a life of introversion on themselves. They close their eyes, they close all their doors and windows, they become like Leibnitz' monads – windowless – then they are bored.

In the marketplace they were fed up, they were

tired, frustrated. It was getting more like a madhouse; they could not find rest. There was too much of relationship and not enough holiday, not enough space to be themselves. They were falling into things, losing their beings. They were becoming more and more material and less and less spiritual. They were losing their direction. They were losing the very consciousness that they are. They escaped. Fed up, frustrated, they escaped. Now they are trying to live alone – a life of introversion. Sooner or later they get bored. Again they have chosen another wing, but again only one wing. This is the way of a lopsided life. They have again fallen into the same fallacy on the opposite pole.

I am neither for this nor for that. I would like you to become so capable that you can remain in the marketplace and yet meditative. I would like you to relate with people, to love, to move in millions of relationships – because they enrich – and yet remain capable of closing your doors and some-times having a holiday from all relationship so that you can relate with your own being also.

Relate with others, but relate with yourself also. Love others, but love yourself also. Go out! – the world is beautiful, adventurous; it is a challenge, it enriches. Don't lose that opportunity! Whenever the world knocks at your door and calls you, go out! Go out fearlessly – there is nothing to lose, there is everything to gain.

But don't get lost. Don't go on and on and get lost. Sometimes come back home. Sometimes forget the world – those are the moments for meditation. Each day, if you want to become balanced, you should balance the outer and the inner. They should carry the same weight, so that inside you never become lopsided.

This is the meaning when Zen masters say: "Walk in the river, but don't allow the water to touch your feet." Be in the world, but don't be of the world. Be in the world, but don't allow the world to be in you. When you come home, you come home – as if the whole world has disappeared.[37]

LIFE IS PURPOSELESS. Don't be shocked. The whole idea of purpose is wrong – it comes out of greed. Life is a sheer joy, a playfulness, a fun, a

meditation is LIVING JOYOUSLY

laughter, to no purpose at all.

Life is its own end, it has no other end. The moment you understand it you have understood what meditation is all about. It is living your life joyously, playfully, totally, and with no purpose at the end, with no purpose in view, no purpose there at all. Just like small children playing on the sea beach, collecting seashells and colored stones – for what purpose? There is no purpose at all.[38]

SOURCES

All footnoted quotations in this book have been taken from the published and unpublished talks of Osho, a 20th-century enlightened mystic.

(1) (unpublished darshan talks) The Golden Wind, Chapter 8

(2) Ancient Music in the Pines, Chapter 7

(3) The Beloved, Volume 1, Chapter 4

(4) Ancient Music in the Pines, Chapter 7

(5) Just Like That,, Chapter 6

(6) The Invitation, Chapter 21

(7) The Ultimate Alchemy, Chapter 16

(8) From Death to Deathlessness, Chapter 16

(9) Come Follow to You, Volume 3, Chapter

(10) Ancient Music in the Pines, Chapter

(11) Philosophia Perennis, Volume 2, Chapter 5

(12) The Empty Boat, Chapter 4

(13) The First Principle, Chapter 4

(14) The Dhammapada, Volume 1, Chapter 7

(15) I Celebrate Myself: God is No Where, Life is Now Here, Chapter 5

(16) The Dhammapada, Volume 1, Chapter 7

(17) *From the False to the Truth*, Chapter 3

(18) *Ancient Music in the Pines*, Chapter 7

(19) *The Dhammapada*, Volume 10, Chapter 1

(20) *Ancient Music in the Pines*, Chapter 7

(21) *The Beloved*, Volume 1, Chapter 4

(22) *Ancient Music in the Pines* #7

(23) *The Book of Wisdom*, Chapter 4

(24) *Ancient Music in the Pines* #7

(25) *Beyond Enlightenment*, Chapter 29

(26) *Dang, Dang, Doko, Dang*, Chapter 5

(27) (unpublished darshan talks) *The Golden Wind*, Chapter 15

(28) *Dang Dang Doko Dang*, Chapter 5

(29) *The Psychology of the Esoteric*, Chapter 2

(30) *Hallelujah! Chapter 15*

(31) *Ah, This! Chapter 2*

(32) *The Pshychology of the Estoteric*, Chapter 2

(33) *The Psychology of the Esoteric*, Chapter 2

(34) *The Heart Sutra* #7

(35) *Ancient Music in the Pines*, Chapter 7

(36) *Ancient Music in the Pines*, Chapter 4

(37) *A Sudden Clash of Thunder*, Chapter #2

(38) *Zen: Zest, Zip, Zap Zing! Chapter 11*

OSHO COMMUNE INTERNATIONAL

The Osho Commune International in Poona, India, guided by his vision, might be described as a laboratory, an experiment in creating the "New Man" - a human being who lives in harmony with himself and his environment, and who is free from all ideologies and belief systems which now divide humanity.

The Commune's Osho Multiversity offers hundreds of workshops, groups and trainings, presented by its nine different faculties.

All these programs are designed to help people to find the knack of meditation: the passive witnessing of thoughts, emotions, and actions, without judgement or identification. Unlike many traditional Eastern disciplines, meditation at Osho Commune is an inseparable part of everyday life - working, relating or just being. The result is that people do not renounce the world but bring to it a spirit of awareness and celebration, in a deep reverence for life.

The highlight of the day at the Commune is the meeting of the Osho White Robe Brotherhood. This two-hour celebration of music, dance and silence, with a discourse from Osho, is unique - a complete meditation in itself where thousands of seekers, in Osho's words, "dissolve into a sea of consciousness."

FOR FURTHER INFORMATION

Many of Osho's books have been translated and published in a variety of languages worldwide. For information about Osho, his meditations, books, tapes, and the address of an Osho meditation/information center near you, contact:

Osho International Foundation
24 St James's Street
London SW1A 1HA, UK

Osho Commune International
17 Koregaon Park
Poona 411001, India